I Am Muhammad Ali

We are the
Black Panthers party.

I am Claudette Colvin

I am Dominique Dawes.

I am Medgar Evers.

I am Evan Forde.

We are the Greensboro Four.

I am Harry Belafonte.

I am Elmer Imes.

I am James W. Johnson.

I am Eartha Kitt.

I am Lewis Latimer.

I am Mary Mcleod Bethune.

I am Reverend
Isaiah DeQuincey Newman.

I am Jesse Owens.

I am Colin Powell.

I am Quincy Jones.

I am Ruby Bridges.

I am Betty Shabazz.

I am Sojourner Truth.

This is the Underground
Railroad.

I am Gustava Vassa.

I am Ida B. Wells.

I am Malcolm X.

I am Andrew Jackson Young.

I am Zora Neal Hurston.